FACES
The Truth of Expression

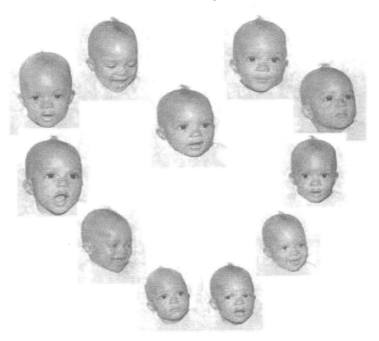

A child's innocence is preserved through love.

Protect me.

Teach Me.

Show me right from wrong.

In return, I **will** make a difference!

1

TO MY FATHER IN HEAVEN: THANK YOU FOR GIVING ME SUCH A WONDERFUL MOTHER AND LOVING DAUGHTER

Ms. Ruth & SJ

CONTENTS

FOREWORD

Take It Personal.

Every person has a story and so does every book.

What does it take for you to take a stand?

What can change the way you feel about love?

What does it take for you to dislike someone?

What event in your life can you reflect upon that directly will cause an emotional rollercoaster in your behavior?

HOW WOULD YOU FEEL?

Your best friend lied to you.

How would you feel if you lost a limb in an accident?

Visualize those events.

What nonverbal body movements cause suspicion towards another?

Is your face a road map to your emotions?

Your nonverbal body movement can reflect your true feelings. Do you have a poker face? What event, what music or what person plainly could cause your nonverbal body movements to reveal what you are feeling?

Have fun while learning new dimensions of yourself.

ACKNOWLEDGEMENTS

As a child, I dreamed of being famous and rich. My mother always told me that Big Dreamers make billionaires. With the completion of this workbook, I realized that I have been a billionaire all my life.

To my mother, Ruth: Tears of joy fill my heart whenever I think of you. Thank you for choosing me as your son. I wish there were two of you so I could share you with the world.

To my daughter SJ: Thank you for teaching me the true meaning of unconditional love. I love you more every second.

Special thanks to the best photographer in the world, Tony Donaldson. You have the eye of a hawk and a heart of gold.

Kimaya Seward. Brains and beauty rolled up in one special lady. God has touched your heart and you have touched mine.

Leonie Walker. Thank you for always giving me the hard truth. You are one of the smartest people I know.

To my dad here on earth: I miss you. Dr. McBride, you may not have been my birth dad, but you were alright with me. I owe you a lot. Hope to see you again one day.

INTRODUCTION

Live truthfully in the moment. It is at that exact time and that exact place you will find what you honestly want to convey.

This is a workbook. Key word **Workbook.** It is designed as an aid to understanding the truth behind an expression through non-verbal communication whether in a business setting or in a relationship. Whether you are an Actor, Lawyer, Doctor, Teacher, Counselor, Police Officer, Athlete, Student, Parent, or whatever your profession, this informative workbook will help you to improve your nonverbal communication skills as well as help you to become a master of expression and interpretation.

In all walks of life, understanding facial expressions can be a key factor between getting it right or getting it wrong.

An expression is worth a thousand words. For a defendant, it can mean the difference between guilt or innocence. For an actor, the command of your facial expression is vital. Although living truthfully in the moment should bring on a natural facial expression, nonverbal communication encompasses so much more.

This is not reading material only, but actual thought-provoking stories, games, questions, examples, and fun interactive exercises.

<u>**CHAPTER 1**</u>

Non-Verbal Communication

Key Notes:

65% of all communication between people is nonverbal. Understanding what your body is saying is essential in all professions. Great public speakers and great actors are keenly aware that body language is equally important as the verbal message. Small movements can get big reviews.

"The body says what words cannot." - *Martha Graham*

Notes:

_____

_____

_____

_____

_____

_____

_____

_____

_____

_____

_____

_____

_____

_____

_____

_____

Non-Verbal Communication

What do these pictures say to you?

Non-verbal communication constitutes 65% of all communication between people. Body language is the primary source of non-verbal communication.

Understanding how your body speaks to others is essential in all areas of public life.

Your non-verbal communication can paint a clear picture about your personality and aid others in "drawing conclusions" about you, whether positive or negative. Most decision makers and people in position to hire understand this explicitly.

Research has shown that employers structure their hiring on the following factors:

    7%   Verbal Communication

    38%   Body Language/Non-Verbal Communication

    55%   Appearance

Non-Verbal Communication

"What you talkin-bout Willis?" was a phrase coined from a hit TV show in the 80's. What are you talking about is a question that is often asked when your actions do not match the words that come from your mouth.

Non-verbal communication covers more than facial expression. Non-verbal communication encompasses gestures, cultural differences, voice intonation, eye contact, expressive body motion, rituals, family values and background, habits, and real-life experiences. To put it simply, "What you say may not be as important as what you do."

What do these pictures say to you?

_____   _____

Understanding Your Face, It's Muscle Location, And The Functionality

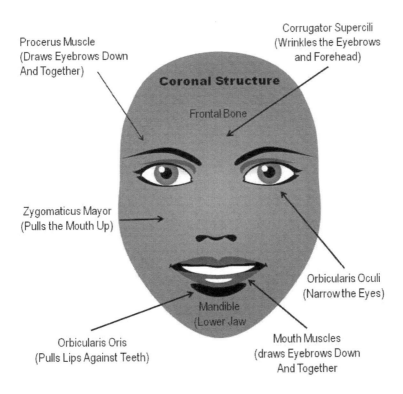

Procerus Muscle
(Draws Eyebrows Down
And Together)

Corrugator Supercili
(Wrinkles the Eyebrows
and Forehead)

Coronal Structure

Frontal Bone

Zygomaticus Mayor
(Pulls the Mouth Up)

Orbicularis Oculi
(Narrow the Eyes)

Mandible
(Lower Jaw

Orbicularis Oris
(Pulls Lips Against Teeth)

Mouth Muscles
(draws Eyebrows Down
And Together

Body Language is a big form of non-verbal communication. Study this picture and write down how many different stories you see?

Notes:

What are they talking about? What is their relationship? What is his body saying? What is her body saying? Email me directly at truthofexpression@gmail.com and tell me the true story behind the picture to receive a free gift.

_____

_____

_____

_____

_____

_____

_____

_____

_____

_____

_____

_____

_____

_____

Public Speaking and Nonverbal Communication

A Professional Speaker Sets the Tone for the Message

As a professional speaker, everything you do the minute you walk into the room sets the tone for your message. Without even speaking one word, you can determine just how many people you will reach because their engagement to your message depends on you and not on them. You can have a great topic to speak about and great presentation skills, but without communicating the passion you have about your topic, none of it really matters!

Get Rid of Distracting Body Movements

Your body movement during your presentation has the ability to strengthen the impact of your message or it can seriously be a distraction. One of your goals as a speaker is to look so natural with your movements and with what you say that no one even notices that you are using intonation and inflection or body movement as a means of emphasizing the points of your speech.

What kinds of mannerisms are distracting?

- Swaying back and forth in front of the audience

- Hanging on to the podium

- Finger tapping

- Licking or biting your lips

- Fidgeting with clothes, pockets, or jewelry

- Frowning

- Fussing with hair

- Bobbing your head

- Flailing arms at inappropriate times

The movements you make during your speech should be planned or at least controlled by you. Any movement that is not planned could potentially be distracting. Many of the above-mentioned mannerisms stem from being nervous about being on stage. Additionally, they could also come just because you don't know you are doing them. Either way, you'll need to minimize and eliminate as many of these movements as possible.

1. Make a video tape of yourself. Do you even know that you are making these movements? Probably not. A video will help you identify which distracting movements you'll need to work on eliminating.

2. Review your video tape for places where you make distracting mannerisms. Make a list of the mannerisms you have and thoughtfully practice your speech without those mannerisms. Rerecord yourself

and keep reviewing your tapes until you are satisfied that all the mannerisms are gone.

3. Work on feeling comfortable with delivering your speech. You should feel natural as you speak about your topic. You should feel like you are sharing information with a long-time friend. This will come when you've spent many hours practicing, reworking, and revising your speech. This will also come because you speak from your heart and let others know the way you feel about your subject.

4. Work on eliminating nervousness when delivering your speech. This will come as you get more familiar with your material. As you take the time to focus on delivering your message instead of focusing on the feelings of fear and anxiety you will notice nervousness fade away.

5. Review your video tapes for places in your speech where you need to add body movements into your presentation that will make it more interesting. Let your movements show the way you feel. These movements should be natural and can work in your favor as you emphasize specific points in your presentation.

6. Body movements should look natural. Consider this when deciding which body movements to incorporate into your presentation. You can use facial expressions and make eye contact with your audience for maximum effects.

Every movement should be planned during your presentation. You can easily lose your audience with distracting movements because their focus and attention will be turned to these movements instead of what you have to say! Go before your audience expecting to make an impact! People aren't interested in what you know. They want your information for themselves, and passion is like the "grease" that lubricates that passage of information! Do you expect that your audience will receive what you have to say? Do you communicate that you're excited to be there and you're also excited that they are there as well?

Change your presentation and tailor it to engage your audience no matter where they might be! Don't stay stuck in a routine! Walk around. Dance if you find it necessary.

Relating to your audience goes beyond just speaking to them. It encompasses everything from the greeting you give, the way you dress and your tone of voice you use to address them. All can be considered parts of non-verbal communication.

You are the key to a successful delivery of your message. If you want to see results, understand that you set the tone whether you are in front of a camera or on stage speaking to thousands of people.

It's up to you to maintain control of that tone!

All professional speakers will need a promotional kit to market themselves effectively and obtain not just more jobs but higher paying ones. Speakers fail to achieve the desired incomes because they fail to properly market their skills and talents. No more failure! Reach the income you've heard and dreamt about by using a promotional kit!

Speaker bureaus and meeting planners expect to see certain pieces of information to see if you are the professional speaker they are looking for. These pieces of information include a content sheet highlighting the material you'll be presenting, a speaker biography, testimonials / reviews, a list of the services you provide including educational materials and fee schedule, a sample client list, a demo video, and a business card with contact information. You can also include a letter on a personalized letterhead stating your interest in the event and why you feel they should choose you. Think Ted Talk as your pot of gold.

1. Content sheet – Include a general outline of the presentation you'll be making. Your material should relate to the theme of the convention or seminar being hosted.

2. Speaker biography (bio) – Highlight certifications and qualifications in your two to three paragraph narrative. Each paragraph should be between two and three sentences and should give bureaus and planners an idea of who you are and what you're about. This bio may also be used as part of the

advertisement of the speaking engagement and may be in the form of a short paragraph. You should also send a picture of yourself.

3. Testimonials / Reviews – This information helps to build your credibility as a speaker because it tells what others are saying about you. In order to build this area effectively, you should also consider requesting feedback after each speaking engagement whether they are free or you charged a fee.

4. List of services and products – This section of information includes a price list of books, CDs, or videos that you produce related to your speaking topic. This section can also include other types of speaking engagements that you do along with the respective prices that you will charge.

5. List of the clients you've worked for – You can combine this with your testimonial and review sections. However, keep in mind that not everyone will respond to your request for feedback. Either you didn't ask for a review or they didn't take the time to fill out your review sheet. You can keep a running list of the people who have used your services.

6. Demo video – This video should be on the subject you are being asked to speak on. It gives your prospective planners an idea of what they will be getting should they choose to hire you. This should also be professionally done.

7. Contact information – Include information on the various ways that speaker bureaus and meeting planners can contact you should they decide to hire you.

Successful marketing ensures that you are on the path to becoming a successful professional speaker. It also presents you as a professional and an established leader in your field. Create your portfolio and get to marketing yourself today!

Remember DO is sometimes better than perfect!

Complete this activity: For (7) days when you awaken in the morning look into the mirror and say, "Wow You Look Great!" Remember your facial response. Look back over the faces you have drawn. Hopefully, you'll have more happy faces than the opposite. Ask yourself why did I feel that way?

Draw the way you feel today in pencil and why with one word

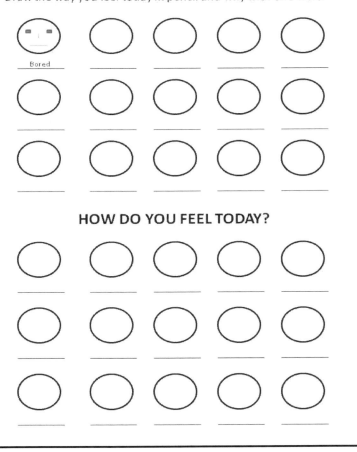

Bored

HOW DO YOU FEEL TODAY?

Complete this activity: For (7) days when you awaken in the morning look into the mirror and say, "Wow You Look Great!" Remember your facial response. Look back over the faces you have drawn. Hopefully, you'll have more happy faces than the opposite. Ask yourself why did I feel that way?

Draw the way you feel today in pencil and why with one word

Bored

HOW DO YOU FEEL TODAY?

Complete this activity: For (7) days when you awaken in the morning look into the mirror and say, "Wow You Look Great!" Remember your facial response. Look back over the faces you have drawn. Hopefully, you'll have more happy faces than the opposite. Ask yourself why did I feel that way?

Draw the way you feel today in pencil and why with one word

Bored

HOW DO YOU FEEL TODAY?

Complete this activity: For (7) days when you awaken in the morning look into the mirror and say, "Wow You Look Great!" Remember your facial response. Look back over the faces you have drawn. Hopefully, you'll have more happy faces than the opposite. Ask yourself why did I feel that way?

Draw the way you feel today in pencil and why with one word

HOW DO YOU FEEL TODAY?

Complete this activity: For (7) days when you awaken in the morning look into the mirror and say, "Wow You Look Great!" Remember your facial response. Look back over the faces you have drawn. Hopefully, you'll have more happy faces than the opposite. Ask yourself why did I feel that way?

Draw the way you feel today in pencil and why with one word

HOW DO YOU FEEL TODAY?

Complete this activity: For (7) days when you awaken in the morning look into the mirror and say, "Wow You Look Great!" Remember your facial response. Look back over the faces you have drawn. Hopefully, you'll have more happy faces than the opposite. Ask yourself why did I feel that way?

Draw the way you feel today in pencil and why with one word

Bored

HOW DO YOU FEEL TODAY?

Complete this activity: For (7) days when you awaken in the morning look into the mirror and say, "Wow You Look Great!" Remember your facial response. Look back over the faces you have drawn. Hopefully, you'll have more happy faces than the opposite. Ask yourself why did I feel that way?

Draw the way you feel today in pencil and why with one word

Bored

HOW DO YOU FEEL TODAY?

APPEARANCE

There was a time when companies would "NOT" hire someone with visually exposed tattoos or if their hair style didn't fit the company image. Today things have changed for the better and for the worse. Publicly, people seem to be less judgmental. However, let's put the old theory on appearance to the test.

Who would you want to meet your parents?

Who would you call for protection?

Who would you ask for business advice?

Who would you trust in a dark alley?

Who would you hire?

Same guy. Do you have preconceived perceptions?

28

CHAPTER 2

Pictures and Diagrams

Key Notes:

A picture can say a thousand words. Here are different words accompanied with pictures and a step-by-step diagram as to how your face might look when feeling a certain emotion.

Live truthfully in the moment and your face will follow.

Likewise, ignoring the way you are truly feeling, and your nonverbal body movement might expose you.

"I'm a world-class people watcher. I like to watch people's body movements, their expressions. It says so much about them." - Jill Scott

Notes:

_____

_____

_____

_____

_____

_____

_____

_____

_____

_____

_____

_____

_____

_____

_____

PICTURES DON'T LIE

It was once said by a pretty wise man that "Kisses Don't Lie".

It was also said that "A Picture can say a thousand words".

What do these pictures say to you?

The birth of your first child!

• The skin on your forehead may be drawn backwards.

• The skin under your eyelids may show some wrinkles.

• The nostrils may or may not be widened.

31

PICTURES DON'T LIE

Anger: Racism.

• Your mouth may or may not be parted.

• If not parted, lips should be tight and tense.

• Your nose should have no wrinkles on it.

• Your eyes should have a fixed hard stare.

PICTURES DON'T LIE

Anger: Racism

- Your mouth may or may not be parted.

- If not parted, lips should be tight and tense.

- Your nose should have no wrinkles on it.

- Your eyes should have a fixed hard stare.

PICTURES DON'T LIE

Hurt/Pain: You just found out your lover has been unfaithful to you

• You need to feel this in the pit of your stomach.

• Try exhaling completely through your nose.

• Hurt/Pain are tricky emotions. Be very aware of your pre-circumstance, because it may trigger a different emotion altogether.

34

PICTURES DON'T LIE

Hurt/Pain: You just found out your lover has been unfaithful to you.

- You need to feel this in the pit of your stomach.

- Try exhaling completely through your nose.

- Hurt/Pain are tricky emotions. Be very aware of your pre-circumstance because it may trigger a different emotion altogether

35

PICTURES DON'T LIE

Confident: Hair perfect, make-up great, I know I'm
looking good today!

• Your eyes should have a fixed stare.

• The eyebrows may be slightly raised.

• Your lips are together or apart slightly.

PICTURES DON'T LIE

Confident: Hair perfect, make-up great, I know I'm

looking good today!

- Your eyes should have a fixed stare.

- The eyebrows may be slightly raised.

- Your lips are together or slightly apart.

PICTURES DON'T LIE

Frightened/Shocked: Fright = Where am I?
Shock = I can't believe you
did that!

• Your eyes are wide open with a fixed stare.

• Your mouth may be parted slightly. If not, lips should be tense.

PICTURES DON'T LIE

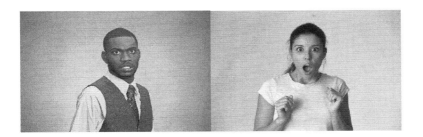

Frightened/Shocked: Fright = Where am I?

Shock = I can't believe you

did that!

- Your eyes are wide open with a fixed stare.

- Your mouth may be parted slightly.

- If not parted, lips should be tense.

PICTURES DON'T LIE

Disgust/Gross: Your neighbor's dog defecates in your yard and you step in it!

• Your upper eyelids are raised with your brows lowered.

• Your cheeks are raised.

• Your nose is wrinkled which might cause a slight tremble on your face.

• Your mouth may or may not be parted.

PICTURES DON'T LIE

Disgust/Gross: Your neighbor's dog pooped in

your yard and you step in it!

- Your upper eyelids are raised with your brows lowered.

- Your cheeks are raised.

- Your nose is wrinkled which causes a slight tremble on

  your face.

- Your mouth may or may not be parted.

- You have an intense eye gaze.

PICTURES DON'T LIE

Ecstatic: You just won the lottery for $20,000,000!

• Your eyebrows should be raised.

• Your forehead may have horizontal wrinkles going across it.

• The corner of your lips should be drawn together.

PICTURES DON'T LIE

Ecstatic: You just won the lottery for $20,000,000!

- Your eyebrows should be raised.

- Your forehead may have horizontal wrinkles going across it.

- The corner of your lips should be drawn together.

PICTURES DON'T LIE

Sad   The loss of a family member or close friend

* The lips are drawn together softly.

* Your eyebrows are drawn downward.

* The skin below the eyebrows is triangulated.

* Your lips may also be trembling (try barely touching your teeth together).

PICTURES DON'T LIE

Sad: The loss of a family member or close friend.

- The lips are drawn together softly.

- Your eyebrows are drawn downward.

- The skin below the eyebrows is triangulated.

- Your lips may also be trembling (try barely touching your teeth together).

PICTURES DON'T LIE

Confusion: Why is Chaos spelled like this?

• One eyebrow may be raised slightly higher than the other.

• Your forehead is slightly wrinkled.

• Your face should be tight and tensed.

• You might say to yourself, "What is he talking about?"

PICTURES DON'T LIE

Confusion: Bewilderment, Perplexity, Uncertain

What do you mean my bank account is overdrawn?

Confusion: Why is Chaos spelled like this?

- Your lips are drawn together.

- If your lips are apart, then your cheekbone should be slightly raised.

- Confusion can also be called "The What Look"

47

PICTURES DON'T LIE

Guilty: You lied in court about a traffic ticket

• Your eyes could be focused downward or upward.

• Your eyebrows are drawn together or raised.

• Your lips are together as to almost say "I'm Sorry" without saying the words.

• Try to raise one eyebrow higher than the other.

PICTURES DON'T LIE

Guilty: You lied in court about a traffic ticket.

- Your eyes could be focused downward or upward.

- Your eyebrows are drawn together or raised.

- Your lips are together as to almost say "I'm Sorry" without saying the words.

PICTURES DON'T LIE

Innocent: Babies,

• Your face should show no wrinkles.

• Your eyes should be sharp and focused.

• You've heard of the puppy dog look.

• Your lips are drawn together and may be pushed out slightly as if giving a soft kiss.

PICTURES DON'T LIE

Innocent: Babies.

- Your face should show no wrinkles.

- Your eyes should be sharp and focused.

- You've heard of the puppy dog look.

- Your lips are drawn together and may be pushed out slightly as if giving a soft kiss.

CHAPTER 3

Word Games

Key Notes:

Interactive exercises for your mind.

Get your mirror ready. You have over 150 different words that you will have to put a face to. Some words may trigger the same emotional reaction. Try your best to use a different facial expression while experiencing the same emotional response to each word.

With practice and dedication, this section should help you obtain instant facial emotional recall.

"Think with the whole body." – Taisen Deshimaru

Notes:

_____

_____

_____

_____

_____

_____

_____

_____

_____

_____

_____

_____

_____

_____

_____

Word Games/Mirror Exercise

Fill in the blanks with your own words.

Use a person's name, a date of an event, or anything that will help you trigger that **EMOTIONAL RESPONSE!**

_____ aggressive	_____ ambitious
_____ analytical	_____ anxious
_____ awful	_____ awkward
_____ bad	_____ bashful
_____ bitter	_____ cunning
_____ certain	_____ combative
_____ concerned	_____ carefree
_____ chatty	_____ clever
_____ caring	_____ confident
_____ classy	_____ clumsy
_____ comical	_____ casual

Word Games/Mirror Exercise
Fill in the blanks with your own words.

Use a person's name, a date of an event, or anything that will help you trigger that
EMOTIONAL RESPONSE

_____ committed   _____ consumed

_____ cowardly   _____ crafty

_____ coy   _____ coward

_____ complex   _____ cordial

_____ conceited   _____ contemplate

_____ cynical   _____ curious

_____ confused   _____ careless

_____ criminal   _____ determined

_____ encourage   _____ excited

_____ eager   _____ exhausted

_____ educated   _____ enraged

Word Games/Mirror Exercise
Fill in the blanks with your own words.

Use a person's name, a date of an event, or anything that will help you trigger that
EMOTIONAL RESPONSE

_____ desperate   _____ determined

_____ confused   _____ careless

_____ dead   _____ dangerous

_____ dread   _____ deaf

_____ diet   _____ direct

_____ depressed   _____ daring

_____ disappoint   _____ driven

_____ established   _____ expressive

_____ elated   _____ endearing

_____ earnest   _____ ebullient

_____ eloquent   _____ electric

Word Games/Mirror Exercise
Fill in the blanks with your own words.

Use a person's name, a date of an event, or anything that will help you trigger that
EMOTIONAL RESPONSE

_____ frightened   _____ frustrated

_____ funny   _____ fragile

_____ forgiving   _____ frank

_____ gloomy   _____ greedy

_____ guilty   _____ generous

_____ graceful   _____ gangster

_____ gay   _____ glad

_____ hateful   _____ hurt

_____ happy   _____ headstrong

_____ honest   _____ hope

_____ impatient   _____ insecure

Word Games/Mirror Exercise
Fill in the blanks with your own words.

Use a person's name, a date of an event, or anything that will help you trigger that
EMOTIONAL RESPONSE

_____ jerk   _____ jealous

_____ kind   _____ judgmental

_____ killer   _____ lazy

_____ lonely   _____ lethargic

_____ mean   _____ miserable

_____ moody   _____ negative

_____ nervous   _____ nurturing

_____ offensive   _____ opinionated

_____ passive   _____ paranoid

_____ pleasant   _____ pressured

_____ pain   _____ passionate

Word Games/Mirror Exercise
Fill in the blanks with your own words.

Use a person's name, a date of an event, or anything that will help you trigger that
EMOTIONAL RESPONSE

_____ ponder   _____ perceptive

_____ possessed   _____ polite

_____ powerful   _____ poor

_____ pretty   _____ pervert

_____ resentful   _____ prejudice

_____ religious   _____ relentless

_____ reflect   _____ rage

_____ relaxed   _____ regret

_____ rich   _____ respectful

_____ romantic   _____ rigid

_____ sexy   _____ run-down

Word Games/Mirror Exercise

Fill in the blanks with your own words.

Use a person's name, a date of an event, or anything that will help you trigger that **EMOTIONAL RESPONSE**

_____ scared	_____ shy
_____ shocked	_____ silly
_____ successful	_____ suspicious
_____ stern	_____ sympathetic
_____ stuffy	_____ spirited
_____ stubborn	_____ secure
_____ smart	_____ superior
_____ sneaky	_____ timid
_____ terrible	_____ upset
_____ tired	_____ unyielding
_____ ugly	_____ vain

Word Games/Mirror Exercise

Fill in the blanks with your own words.

Use a person's name, a date of an event, or anything that will help you trigger that
EMOTIONAL RESPONSE

_____ valor	_____ unemployed
_____ vigilant	_____ urgent
_____ virgin	_____ vigorous
_____ voracious	_____ victimize
_____ vulgar	_____ violent
_____ victorious	_____ vivacious
_____ warm	_____ vulnerable
_____ witty	_____ worried
_____ worthless	_____ winner
_____ weep	_____ wicked
_____ wrong	_____ wise

<u>CHAPTER 4</u>

Expressions

Key Notes:

What do these expressions say to you?

Fill in the blanks with your opinions and feelings about what you see. Match a word with the corresponding expression and write a brief note for recall.

After mastering this section, you should be able to give yourself a pre-circumstance for any situation.

"The movement of the body is where poetry begins." - Clint Catalyst

---

Notes:

_____

_____

_____

_____

_____

_____

_____

_____

_____

_____

_____

_____

_____

_____

_____

_____

_____

What do these expressions say to you?

_____   _____

Notes: _____

_____

_____

_____

_____

*

*

*

*

What do these expressions say to you?

_____   _____

Notes: _____

_____

_____

_____

_____

*

*

*

*

65

What do these expressions say to you?

 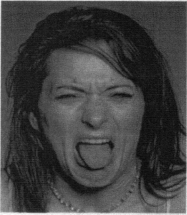

_____   _____

Notes: _____

_____

_____

_____

_____

*

*

*

*

What do these expressions say to you?

_____   _____

Notes: _____

_____

_____

_____

_____

*

*

*

*

What do these expressions say to you?

_____   _____

Notes: _____

_____

_____

_____

_____

-
-
-
-

What do these expressions say to you?

_____   _____

Notes: _____

_____

_____

_____

_____

-
-
-
-

What do these expressions say to you?

_____   _____

Notes: _____

_____

_____

_____

_____

•

•

•

•

What do these expressions say to you?

_____   _____

Notes: _____

_____

_____

_____

_____

•

•

•

•

What do these expressions say to you?

_____   _____

Notes: _____

_____

_____

_____

_____

-
-
-
-

What do these expressions say to you?

_____   _____

Notes: _____

_____

_____

_____

_____

*

*

*

*

What do these expressions say to you?

_____   _____

Notes: _____

_____

_____

_____

_____

•

•

•

•

What do these expressions say to you?

_____   _____

Notes: _____

_____

_____

_____

_____

-
-
-
-

<u>CHAPTER 5</u>

Thought Provoking

Key Notes:

How do you really feel? Make it personal.

Does your personal feeling about a person, place or thing affect your facial expression?

After mastering this section, you should be able to change your facial expression using one word, create a pre-circumstance, and have great topics to discuss with friends.

"Let your body move. It will give voice to a language that can heal." - Gina Greenlee

Notes:

_____

_____

_____

_____

_____

_____

_____

_____

_____

_____

_____

_____

_____

_____

_____

_____

_____

_____

THINGS THAT MAKE YOU GO HMMMM!
(Remember how you feel after you read each line)

Female sports being coached by men only? _____

How do you feel about female entertainers receiving lower pay? _____

Graduation day? _____

Being in love? _____

Where were you and how did you feel about the assassination of:

 Martin Luther King Jr.?_____

President John F. Kennedy?_____

Have you ever been in love with someone and wondered why? _____

Student athletes should not have to take finals during sports season?_____

Cheating on school exams? _____

How do you feel about your favorite teacher? _____

Females who don't cook should never get married?

_____

How do you feel about your grandfather?

_____

THINGS THAT MAKE YOU GO HMMMM!
(Remember how you feel after you read each line)

Woman driving while putting on make-up? _____

Asian drivers? _____

A father and his daughter? _____

Summer vacations? _____

Girl Scouts?_____

Boy Scouts? _____

How do you feel about the Red Cross? _____

Your bank account being overdrawn? _____

Your Job? _____

Your dream job? _____

Hospital test? _____

Cigarettes kill? _____

Your pet ran away? _____

Your favorite meal. _____

People without medical coverage? _____

Do you have more bills than money? _____

Asian people are the smartest race? _____

THINGS THAT MAKE YOU GO HMMMM!
(Remember how you feel after you read each line)

Have you ever had a friend that was in love with a total jerk? _____

It's a man's right to do whatever he wants? _____

My partner thinks I am faithful, I'm not? _____

If I take the life of another, will I still go to heaven?
_____

Is there a Heaven? _____

All thin people should eat more? _____

Comedians make better actors? _____

A hot shower? _____

Getting junk mail? _____

If you kill a bad person does that make you a bad person? _____

Rappers never use drugs? _____

Laughing so hard that your face hurts? _____

Country music rocks? _____

A hot bubble bath? _____

Taking a drive in the country? _____

Can Christians be cremated? _____

THINGS THAT MAKE YOU GO HMMMM!
(Remember how you feel after you read each line)

Hearing your favorite song on the radio on a rainy day? _____

Cannabis should be legal to use? _____

All professional athletes are heroes? _____

How do you feel about Asian Americans? _____

911? _____

Rainbows? _____

Jewish People? _____

African Americans? _____

The President of the United States? _____

Your first kiss? _____

How do you feel about gossip? _____

Spending times with old friends? _____

Running barefoot on the beach? _____

Hot apple pie? _____

Ice cream and cake? _____

BBQ? _____

Flying on an airplane? _____

THINGS THAT MAKE YOU GO HMMMM!
(Remember how you feel after you read each line)

Finding money in your pocket? _____

All lawyers are honest? _____

Having someone wash your hair? _____

Deaf people driving a car? _____

Public toilets? _____

Drug use? _____

Your health? _____

Cigar smoke? _____

Using your cell phone while driving? _____

Playing with a new puppy? _____

Homeless people? _____

Winning the lottery? _____

Watching the sunset? _____

Going to a concert with your best friend? _____

Having to use public transportation? _____

I'm homeless and eat out of the trash? _____

Only rich people should live in Beverly Hills? _____

Everyone in jail is guilty? _____

CHAPTER 6

Things to Be Aware of

Key Notes:

Slouching down in your chair.
Excessive Blinking.

Squirming or not looking a person in the face when you are speaking to them.

What may these things convey to others watching you?

"When you step back and watch people, you realize that we use every single body part. Movement, dance - I find it genius because it's ultimate expression, really." - Jude Law

Notes:

_____

_____

_____

_____

_____

_____

_____

_____

_____

_____

_____

_____

_____

_____

_____

_____

Things to be Aware of

Look at what these examples could mean to others.

1. Slouched down in your chair.

   "I am not interested in anything you have to say."
   "I am tired."
   "My energy level is very low."
   "Is this interview over yet?"

2. Excessive Blinking.

   "I am doubtful of my ability."
   "I am guilty or undecided."
   "I am worried."
   "I have something in my eye."
   "I am tired and stressed."

3. Squirming in your chair.

   "I am very uncomfortable."
   "I can't take the pressure."
   "I have to go to the restroom."
   "I should have worn different underpants."

4. Avoiding eye contact while speaking.

   "I am not trustworthy."
   "I am shy."
   "I am scared of you."
   "I have something to hide."

Things to be Aware of
How would the person in each situation look?

You have a major crush on your best friend.

My significant other was unfaithful.

I am not comfortable with talking to you.

I am not a good liar, but I had to lie for the job.

I must use the restroom right now.

Your mother-in-law's dinner was horrible.

I found $500.00 dollars at the gym.

I finished my assignment early now I can party.

My stomach hurts because I'm nervous.

I accidently hit the dog and it died.

Understand how you feel about a certain event, moment, or person can change. Today thinking about my father's passing saddens me because it's his birthday. Last week thinking about my father's passing brought a smile to my face because I saw a video of him laughing as he skateboarded into a pile of garbage.

Recommended Tools
(Never leave home without them)

Actor

1. Extra head shots and resume
2. Change for the parking meter
3. Change of clothes
4. Make-Up and Mirror
5. Breath mints
6. Eye Drops
7. Cell Phone
8. Book to read (Faces The Truth of Expression)

Photographer

1. Extra Batteries
2. Extra Flash Care or SD
3. Make-Up
4. Cell Phone
5. Towels or Baby Wipes
6. Extra Camera

Model

1. Hair Accessories
2. Extra Make-Up
3. Needle & Thread
4. Cell Phone with GPS
5. Change of Clothes
6. Portfolio
7. Comfortable Shoes
8. Money for Acts of Nature

Recommended Tools
(Never leave home without them)

Professional Speaker/Motivator

1. Business Cards
2. Miniature Tape Recorder
3. Overhead Projector/Laptop
4. Visual Aids
5. Pointer
6. Cell Phone
7. Bottled Water
8. Breath Mints

Employment Seeker

1. Positive Attitude
2. Have A Smile In Your Voice
3. Identification
4. Resumes
5. Extra Black & Blue Ink Pen
6. Cell Phone With GPS
7. Good Luck

Internet Presentation

1. Backup notes
2. Do tech prep
3. Backup computer or cell phone
4. Check your background
5. Find a comfortable noise free location
6. Have fun

CHAPTER 7

Internet Presentation

Key Notes:

Change is a part of life. You can either accept it or crawl under a rock and hope for the best. Today, understanding how to navigate the internet to communicate is no longer an option. Auditioning, Employment, and Education, for now are primarily done online. Master your internet online presentation and change your life.

"Trying out new ways of using your body in handling various situations breaks you free from old ways of thinking and being." – Mirka Knaster

Notes:

_____

_____

_____

_____

_____

_____

_____

_____

_____

_____

_____

_____

_____

_____

_____

_____

When auditioning or giving a presentation using any internet platform you must try to master your body movement.

- Practice or rehearse before every audition or presentation.
- Own your space.
- Be alive in your box.
- "KISS" less is best 90% of the time.
- Try to keep your notes and scripts at lens level.
- Turn off your cell phone, audio, and notification chime.
- Master the subtle body movements.
- Understand that your voice conveys a message.
- Replace "um" with a word. Slow Down.
- Make love to the camera.
- Invest in a ring light.
- Pay your internet bill.
- Have a backup plan or second computer.

Remember the basics. Your eyes can create a look of passion, anger, confusion, or nothing at all. In the 2010 movie The Tourist, I was totally captivated by Angelina Jolie's subtle eye gaze and softly spoken words. She completely owned her space and mastered her body movements. I found myself falling in love with her character. I was mesmerized and drawn to her every movement. Her walk was seductive and alluring. Her subtle eye gaze drew me in like a lion fixated on his pray. I was all hers.

When auditioning in front of a casting director, producer or giving a presentation in front of a large audience you have your whole body to help you convey the meaning of words spoken from your mouth. You must be alive in your box. Allow your facial expressions, voice intonation, and nonverbal skills decipher your body language and bring life to your words.

Excessive blinking can signify a feeling of comfortability, stress, or you may only have dry eyes which need some good sleep or eye drops. A blink of an eye with a smirk and a slight head nod can mean I agree or disagree just as that same eye blink with a soft smile can be very seductive or flirtatious.

Your voice is a big part of your nonverbal body language which may sound like an oxymoron. Speaking in a whisper can convey intrigue and curiosity, but you may also sound unsure or show a lack of confidence.

To many people, using the word "um" can kill a great presentation. Slow down and replace the "um" with a word. Pacing normally refers to the rate of speed at which one walks however pacing has an important function when talking about speech or voice. Conversational pace which is used when public speaking ranges from one hundred forty to one hundred seventy words per minute. If you are speaking slower than one hundred forty words per minute, your audience may lose interest in you, what you are saying, and what you are selling.

I received my bachelor's degree in speech from the University of Hawaii. I have a BS degree in speech. Thinking about that makes me laugh. I have a "BS" in speaking. I'm sure I would have been a great politician. I received my SAG card over twenty years ago. I've been on almost every soap opera and a few television shows. Close-up toothpaste was my favorite commercial. I had to kiss over twenty five different ladies for the audition before I booked the lead spot. Twenty-five different ladies with no mouth wash or mints in between. Look it up on YouTube and watch my skills. I mention these events or parts of my life not to brag but to show that writing this book was not only based on research, but also practical hands-on experience.

When I think about captivating internet presentations and great motivational speakers two of my favorites come to mind: Steve Harvey and Mel Robbins. Both of whom played a significant part in changing my life. Mel Robbins' concept of 5,4,3,2,1 is so simple. I couldn't believe it worked until I applied it to my life. After reading Steve Harvey's book Jump, I quit my job, moved to a new state, and started writing my first book. I wish I could say everything was great after I jumped but it wasn't at first. I almost lost everything I owned. The people at the pawn shop knew me by first name. The great thing about jumping though, was I found my purpose and I never looked back. Mr. Harvey said the two most important days of your life are the day you were born and the day you find out why.

I have a dream to be on stage giving this amazing Ted talk speech. I have no idea what the topic will be. However, what I'm going to show you is how action and preparation can assist with manifestation. What is your purpose? I have taken Storytelling classes, voice over training at SAG-AFTRA, and acting workshops from the amazing casting director Amy Jo Berman. I studied The Sanford Meisner technique at Playhouse West under Robert Carnegie and actor producer Jeff Goldblum. I've watched and studied the style and presentation skills of hundreds of TED Talk presenters. I am an amazing storyteller. I believe I am one of the best. Not because I have a degree in speech, or the fact that I have taken storytelling classes. No, I am a great storyteller because I love it. Training is an absolute however I believe Do is better than perfect. When you find your purpose everyday will be a day worth living. Find your purpose and get busy living.

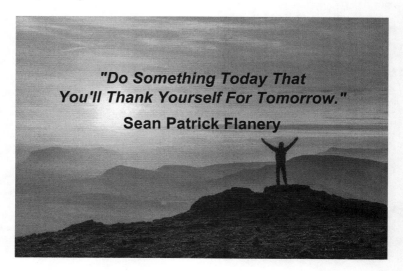

"Do Something Today That You'll Thank Yourself For Tomorrow."

Sean Patrick Flanery

CHAPTER 8

Notes

Key Notes:

In this section you have an opportunity to write your thoughts and feelings about your expressions and the expressions of others. Try to be observant of the faces around you. You can refer to these notes later to sharpen your skills and use as a quick reference.

"Sign is a live, contemporaneous, visual-gestural language and consists of hand shapes, hand positioning, facial expressions, and body movements. Simply put, it is for me the most beautiful, immediate, and expressive of languages, because it incorporates the entire human body." - Myron Uhlberg

Faces The Truth of Expression

Notes:

_____

_____

_____

_____

_____

_____

_____

_____

_____

_____

_____

_____

_____

_____

_____

_____

In the end

This is what it is all about:

Mind, Body, Soul, Humanity, Humility, and Love for one another!

Motivational Quotes

1. 'The only place where success comes before work is in the dictionary.' – Vidal Sassoon
2. 'Whether you think you can, or you think you can't, you're right.' – Henry Ford
3. 'Action is the foundational key to all success.' – Pablo Picasso
4. 'If you let people's perception of you dictate your actions you will have difficulty growing as a person. Be of service, walk your own path. Big dreamers make Billionaires.' – Me
5. 'The best time to plant a tree was 20 years ago. The second-best time is now.' – Chinese proverb
6. 'What would you attempt to do if you knew you would not fail?' – Robert Schuller
7. 'Doing nothing for others is the undoing of ourselves.' – Horace Mann
8. 'When your body surrenders to movement, your soul remembers it's dance.' – Gabrielle Roth

What is your favorite quote? What motivates you to do better? How much time do you spend with your family? How much time is too much time?

About the Author

Delrae Hemphill is an author, playwright, successful businessman, and actor.

He is one of the most creative and determined people you'll ever meet. The creativity within him is apparent the minute you pick up his book. His love for the arts and constant pursuit of excellence inspired him to write this informative, thought-provoking, and fun workbook.

Not being a perfectionist but understanding perfection, Delrae continues to challenge and motivate others to accept and welcome change. His approach to life can be characterized with three words: Integrity, loyalty, and faith.

If you ask Delrae what he feels to be his biggest achievement so far in life his answer would be very simple: Being a dad to his teenage daughter SJ.

If big "Dreamers" make billionaires, then Get Ready, Get Ready, Get Ready. Delrae's best is yet to come!!

Made in the USA
Columbia, SC
22 July 2022

63844096R00054